HOW TO SURVIVE HIGH SCHOOL

D1561459

HOW TO SURVIVE HIGH SCHOOL

A STUDENT'S GUIDE

by Terry Dunnahoo

Illustrated by Tom Huffman

Franklin Watts
New York/Chicago/London/Toronto/Sydney

Best to Brian Thomas,
from Uncle Tom
—T.H.

Library of Congress Cataloging-in-Publication Data

Dunnahoo, Terry.
How to survive high school : a student's guide / by Terry
Dunnahoo.
p.   cm.
Includes bibliographical references (p.   ) and index.
Summary: Provides advice for those entering high school, covering
such topics as friendship, choice of courses, and goals after
graduation.
ISBN 0-531-11135-0
1. High school students—United States—Juvenile literature.
2. High school students—United States—Conduct of life—Juvenile
literature. 3. High school students—United States—Psychology—
Juvenile literature. [1. High schools. 2. Schools.] I. Title.
LA229.D86   1993
373.18—dc20   92-41700 CIP AC

First Paperback Edition 1994
0-531-15705-9

To my nephew Mark
with love
—T.D.

CONTENTS

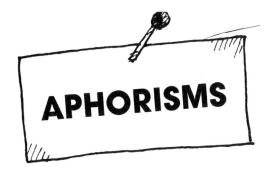

APHORISMS

"A child miseducated is a child lost."

JOHN F. KENNEDY

"The secret of education is respecting the pupil."

RALPH WALDO EMERSON

"Education is hanging around until you've caught on."

ROBERT FROST

"Education is the best provision for old age."

ARISTOTLE

"Education is a weapon whose effect depends on who holds it in his hands and at whom it is aimed."

JOSEPH STALIN

"Upon the subject of education. . . I can only say that I view it as the most important subject that we, as a people, can engage in. . . ."

ABRAHAM LINCOLN

"Sixty years ago I knew everything; now I know nothing; education is a progressive discovery of our own ignorance."

WILL DURANT

"Education is what's left over after you've forgotten the facts."

ANON.

TO THE READER

I was the first person in my family to graduate from high school. And I had to beg my parents to let me graduate. It wasn't because they didn't believe education was important. They did. But they worked in cotton mills ten hours a day, and there still wasn't enough money to take care of necessities. So everybody in my family had to go to work as soon as he or she could legally get a job.

My older siblings worked part-time at fourteen and full-time at sixteen. I also worked part-time at fourteen but, as my sixteenth birthday approached, I didn't want to leave school. I believed a high school diploma would give me a better life. So I promised my parents if they'd let me stay in school, I'd work after class, on weekends, and during the summer, and I'd give them all the money I earned. They agreed.

Sometimes I had one job at a time, and sometimes I had two. During my junior year I had three. When the dismissal bell rang, I raced out of class to a factory that made airplane engines. Three nights a week I raced home from the factory to eat dinner and raced to a movie theater to sell tickets. On weekends, I sold tickets at a roller skating rink.

Every penny I earned I gave to my parents, and they gave me the few dollars they could spare.

The worst job was during the summers. While other kids went to the beach, I went to work in a sweatshop eight hours a day. This was a deafening place with 200 sewing machines running all at once. There was no air-conditioning and temperatures soared over 100 degrees F. I was paid by the piece which meant the more dress seams I sewed, the more money I made. If I didn't make my quota, I'd lose my job which meant I'd have to drop out of high school. Did I ever want to quit? Yes. But I kept my mind on my dream of a better life.

During my high school years, I didn't think of being a writer. In fact, I had no idea what I wanted to be. But I knew I didn't want to spend my life making airplane engines, selling tickets, or working in sweatshops. So when I graduated, I applied for a job at an attorney's office. Because of my diploma and my work experience, I got the job. From there, I worked for the U.S. Navy Department on Guam, a job that took me 9,000 miles (14,484 km) from home.

Guam was my first trip outside the continental United States, and it gave me a love of travel. The introduction to other cultures expanded my interests and has helped me with my writing. But what really helped me with my writing was what I learned in high school. I took Latin and French which helped me understand the origin of words. I learned the use of grammar and studied literature. And I learned to type; a skill every writer should have.

I wrote this book, *How To Survive High School*, to help you make decisions. The classes you take will be different from mine. Your experiences through high school will certainly be different.

Maybe you'll go to college. Whatever you do, re-member that learning never stops. It enhances your life with twists and turns you never dreamed were there. My twists and turns made me a writer.

TERRY DUNNAHOO

HIGH SCHOOL
AND YOU

You stand in lines to get tickets to see your favorite rock group. You stand in line to get into the concert building. You stand in line to get food and drinks. And you often do it without complaining. Why? Because you will be part of an adventure.

On the first day of high school, you may find another line. And for what? More studying, more books, and more teachers' dirty looks?

Did you complain when you stood in line for five hours to see your favorite rock star? Probably not. So do not complain if you have to stand in line for classes on the first day of high school. You are on another adventure. This one will not have you dancing in the aisles, but it will change your life—for better or for worse. The choice is yours.

It seems as though you have been in school forever. You cannot remember everything that happened during all those years. And you probably do not remember the day you started kindergarten. But you probably remember your first day at junior high. Remember all those rooms you had to find about every fifty minutes? Sometimes, changing classes was scary.

Now that you are in high school you have to

find rooms again. And every time you walk into a room, you have to face a new teacher. Is she the one who will fail you? Is he the one who will talk on and on without saying anything you are interested in? Is she the one who will become your friend?

And who are all those kids looking for rooms? In elementary school, you knew most of the students. They lived in your neighborhood. You saw them on the way to school and on the way home. You were in the same class all day. You knew which kids would give you a hard time and which were your friends. In junior high, things were a bit different. You did not know everybody but chances are many of your friends went from elementary school to junior high with you, so you still had friends to hang out with.

You were lucky then. Maybe you are lucky now. If you live in a small city, you may be with kids you were with in kindergarten. But if you live in a big city, you are probably not so lucky. Maybe kids are bused to your school from other parts of the area. Maybe you are bused to an area on the other side of the city. Busing usually means kids you do not know.

Change is scary, and it can do scary things to your body. A boy dreaded going to high school so much, he became sick enough for his parents to take him to a doctor. The doctor examined the boy and found nothing wrong. The doctor ran medical tests. No disease showed up.

Still the boy woke up every morning with pains in his stomach. When his parents insisted he go to school anyway, the boy had trouble breathing. His parents took him back to the doctor. More tests showed the boy was physically healthy. His pains

and problem with breathing were real in his mind but not real in his body.

After sympathetic understanding from his parents and a determination to get over his "illness," the boy could get through a few hours of school. He had learned where his classes were; he liked some of his teachers and had made friends. Within a few weeks he was going to school all day, every day. If this boy had prepared himself for high school, maybe he would not have been so scared with the changes, and he would not have experienced all that pain.

What happened to this boy was one way of dealing with change. On the other hand, there are people who do not worry much about changing schools. A girl whose mother was in the military moved so often, she hardly gave a second thought to her first day of high school. You are probably less worried than the boy and more worried than the girl.

✒ YOU ARE NOT ALONE

Millions of people survive the first day of high school every year. The better prepared you are, the easier it is to get through the first few days. So take advantage of what your school offers:

1. If your school invites senior high students or counselors to visit your junior high, go to the meetings and pay attention to what they say.

2. If you are invited to visit the high school, you should go.

3. If there is an assembly at the high school before classes begin, go. You will be told what to expect from the school and what the school expects from you. You may also receive a packet with maps that show classrooms, lockers, cafeteria, and bathrooms. After the assembly, walk through the campus to find these places.

4. On the first day of school, there will be signs telling you where to check in. Some schools have students give directions. They will answer your questions. Ask. They will not think you are stupid if you ask questions.

5. If you get lost, you will not be alone. Look around. People go in one direction then another and back in the direction they were going in the first place. Maybe you are too shy to ask for directions. And maybe you still believe people think you are dumb if you ask for help. Chances are the kid you ask is searching for the same room you are looking for, and you can hunt for it together. You will not only find the room faster, you may also find a friend.

If a friend transferred with you from junior high to senior high, you already have a friend. But an extra one will not hurt. In fact, that new friend may be in your classes and your best friend may not. Besides, who says you cannot have more than one friend?

A smile can start a friendship. A question can start a friendship. An answer can start a friendship. So do not always wait for somebody else to make the first move. Let people know you are interested in them.

Ask them what junior high school they are from. Ask them where they live. They may ride the same

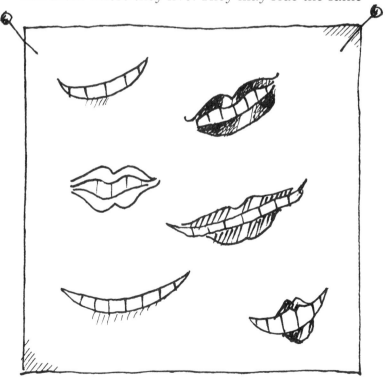

bus you do. They may walk home in the same direction you do. Ask them what music group they like. What is their favorite movie? Do they have a hobby? What do they do for fun? Look interested in what they say. By the time you get the answers to some of those questions, you may not have a friend, but you may have acquaintances.

Will these acquaintances become your friends? Maybe they will, or maybe they will just be somebody in some of your classes. That's okay. Nobody can be best friends with every kid in school.

Will you be popular? Maybe. Maybe not. If you knew the secret to popularity, you could sell a *How-to-Be-Popular* video and make enough money to pay for your college education. But there is not any secret formula to popularity. There is not even a definition everybody can agree on.

Some people think popularity is having a souped-up car, having the most video games, or throwing the greatest parties. Is popularity being great looking, wearing the best clothes, having a sense of humor? All of these help, unless you brag so much about them you become obnoxious.

If you have any of these things going for you, terrific. If you do not, it does not mean you cannot be popular. If you just be yourself instead of trying to act like somebody else, if you are not always putting people down, if you help people, chances are you will have friends. And having friends is what most people agree makes somebody popular.

A quick way to make friends is to go out for sports. If you are not into sports, join clubs. Do you like to play chess? Do you like to take pictures? Do you like languages? Do you like acting? Do you collect stamps? Do you collect baseball cards? Do you collect bugs? If you are not interested in any of the clubs the school offers, other

kids may feel the same way. Ask around. Maybe you can start a new club. Maybe you can be president of the club.

Kids who belong to clubs often get together after school to study, for parties, or to hang out. When you belong to clubs, your chance of making friends zooms. Some of the kids you meet may be the most popular in the school, and you will become part of their group. But do not join a club just because the most popular kids in school belong to it. It is better to be popular in a group of people you have a lot in common with than to be in a group where you feel you do not belong.

Maybe you will not get a date on your first day in high school. Maybe you will not fall in love with a class. Maybe you will not find out where you belong. But think of the search as another stepping-stone in your life. Whether you go up the steps or down the steps is up to you.

WHAT ARE YOUR GOALS?

Some kids decide when they are very young what they will do when they grow up. A four-year-old says she wants to be a doctor because her doctor gives her lollipops. A five-year-old says he wants to be a fire fighter. He decided that when there was a fire in his neighborhood, and he thought it would be fun to ride on a fire truck. A seven-year-old says he wants to be a farmer because his father is a farmer.

Children say they want to be all kinds of things. Some change their mind every day. Some change their mind every week. Some never change their mind. What they wanted to be at four, five, or seven, they still want to be after they grow up.

But most kids do not think seriously about their future. Young people are more *now* oriented than *future* oriented. So if you are about to enter high school, or if you are already there and you do not know what kind of work you want to do as an adult, you are normal. But you probably want to start thinking about your future.

❦WHICH WAY TO GO?

> "My parents want me to be a lawyer but I don't want to be a lawyer. Nag, nag, nag. They never stop nagging about it."

If you feel this way, ask yourself why you are so much against being a lawyer. Is it because you definitely do not want to be a lawyer? Or is it because your parents nag you so much? Sometimes people rebel at something they want to do just because somebody is trying to pressure them.

To help you come up with the right answer, talk to your counselor or to a teacher you feel will give you an honest opinion. Maybe you can talk to friends or relatives who are not part of the pressure. You may decide you are not rebelling against the nagging. You simply do not want to be what your parents want you to be. Then do not give in to the pressure. Career decisions can affect your whole life.

On the other hand, career decisions do not tie you down forever. Years ago people thought the career they chose when they were young was the work they would do for the rest of their lives. Now, people have two, three, or more careers before they retire. Some never retire.

Maybe your family is not pressuring you to enter a certain profession. Instead, they have all kinds of suggestions about what you should do with your life. If you all agree about what you should do, you do not have a problem. But if your parents want you to be a dentist but you want to be an astronaut, and you have not yet told them, it is time to get serious.

Before you tell your family you want to be the first settler on Mars, you should know what you will have to do before you can reach your goal. Astronauts have to pass a lot of math and other science courses. If you hate these subjects and never get anything higher than a C in them, you may want to stop bickering with your family about being an astronaut. But if you never get anything higher than a C, even though you like these subjects, there may still be hope for your dream of flying through space.

Maybe you get low grades because you have not worked hard enough to get higher grades. This is easy to solve. Work harder. Maybe you never quite understood some of the science theories. If this is the reason for the Cs, talk to your teacher and ask for help, or ask your parents to hire a tutor to help you.

Maybe you do not want to be an astronaut. Maybe you want to be a mechanic, but your parents want a dentist in the family. They say you have too much intelligence and talent to waste your life working on cars. But maybe your talent is that you can pick up a sour note in an engine as fast as you can hear a sour note at a rock concert. If you can, you have a special talent.

Talent does not always mean what others think it means. And intelligence can not always be measured by the kinds of tests you have been given almost from the day you started school. People are gifted in different ways. Maybe your way is building a mall on Mars. Maybe your gift is taking apart an engine that will not turn over and then putting it back together so it runs as well as it did when it was new. Maybe your gift is being a clown or a salesperson or a football player.

Maybe your talent is expressing yourself through dance, drama, art, or music. After three years of struggling with every subject except art, one student found a teacher who encouraged her talent. Through this teacher's help, the student stopped feeling like a square peg in a round hole. At graduation she was asked how she felt.

"I'm going to the School of the Arts. The world is beautiful."

Suppose people do not think you can be an artist, a dentist, an astronaut, or a mechanic? Suppose you have the kind of parents who think you will never amount to anything? They say you are a goof-off. They say you are clumsy. They say you are stupid and you can not learn things as fast as other kids. If they have been saying these kinds of things all your life, you probably believe them. If your parents keep putting you down, it may be harder to reach your goals than it will be for kids who have families who praise and encourage them. But keep telling yourself you can be anything you want to be. Your determination will help you reach your goals.

On the other hand, there is some danger in getting too much praise. If your parents praise you for everything you do, you may think you are so great, you can walk into a class and ace any test without studying. You may think it is okay to go to the beach instead of going to school. How much harm will missing an occasional day of school make?

Suppose that is the day your science teacher explains the formula you have trouble with. Not knowing a basic formula can mess up future experiments. Ditching is not the way to reach your goals.

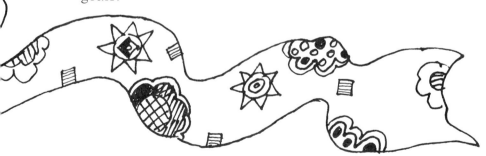

✴ RIGHT BRAIN, LEFT BRAIN, WHICH BRAIN?

You only have one brain. People who study how the brain works agree on this. They also agree the two parts of the brain are connected. The connections carry messages between the two parts. And each part controls movements on opposite sides of the body.

· If you turn on MTV with your right hand, the left part of the brain had to send the message to your right hand before you could do it. If you make a left-handed throw to third base and pick off the runner, the right side of your brain sent the message to your left hand.

Researchers say people are right brain or left brain. According to them, the left brain controls logic and language, and the right brain controls imagination and creativity. Some researchers also say that, although each side works, one side dominates the other. Not everyone agrees with this. In

28

fact, there is evidence that says after one side of the brain has dominated for a while, it gives the other side a chance to dominate. This evidence shows that both sides of your brain can work together.

So if you were tested and were told you are right brain or left brain, do not let the "label" discourage you from reaching your goal. If you want to be an engineer and you have been labeled *right brain*, remember that your left brain is not snoozing. It stays wide awake and is ready to help you. If you want to be an artist and you have been labeled *left brain*, keep in mind your right brain will not abandon you. Most of all, remember labels are not always right.

OTHER LABELS

Some labels that educators often use for students are *underachievers, achievers,* and *overachievers.* According to these labels, underachievers are students who have been identified as being able to do certain work, but who are not doing it as well as they should. Achievers are students who have been identified as being able to do certain work and are doing it as well as they should. Overachievers are students who have been identified as being able to do certain work and usually do it better than other students.

One of these labels may already be in the school records that follow you from grade to grade and school to school. Some teachers will believe your label. Some will give you a chance to prove your label wrong.

You should have that chance. It is not fair to be judged by something you did in third or fourth grade, or whatever grade you messed up in. Maybe there was something wrong with your health. Maybe your parents were getting a divorce. Maybe you had to move to another city. Maybe English is not your first language, and the tests you took were in English. Whatever the reason you were labeled, you have the right to know what your label is.

In the past, only school administrators, teachers, and sometimes the police could look at your records. But now under the Freedom of Information Act, you and your parents can examine your school records. If there is something in them you feel is unfair, you can ask your school administrators to take it out.

If you ask for a hearing, the administrators must hear your complaint. If they do not agree that something in your record should be taken out, the information will stay. But your challenge will also go into the record. This will probably help you more than it will hurt you. So challenge. What is in your records could affect your chances of getting into college.

⋙ ALTERNATIVE EDUCATION

A way to reach your goal may be to go to an alternative school, a private school, a parochial school, a magnet school, or study at home.

Alternative schools are public schools that create their own rules. To do this, administrators must get permission from members of the school board to run the schools differently than other schools in that area.

Alternative schools often do not have strict schedules, do not give report cards, and let kids choose projects they want to work on. If you love poetry and music, you may not have to create a science project. If you want to build skyscrapers, you may be allowed to draw plans in class instead of going to gym. And there may be no bells to interrupt your thinking. Alternative schools do not interrupt your creativity by ringing bells so you can go to another class.

Does this sound like alternative schools were created just for you? Before you race to register, ask yourself if you are mature enough to work on your own. Just because the law says you are no longer a minor, does not mean you are mature. A lot of adults are immature in their thinking and in their actions. Maturity for alternative schools means you have the discipline and the ability to work without people always telling you to get to work.

Since you started kindergarten you have been told when to open your book, when to take out your pencil, when to go to recess. Some people need to be told what to do. If you need to be told what to do, stay in your more traditional school. If you think you are mature enough for an alternative school, ask your counselor if there is one in your city. If there is, talk to your parents about going. You may get a "no." Most people think traditional schools are the only way to get an education. But if you, your family, your counselor, and teachers agree you should go to an alternative school, try it.

What if you find you cannot handle the freedom of choices that an alternative school gives you? No sweat. You can go back to the high school you left.

Some areas have magnet schools. Rules in magnet schools are usually not as strict as in traditional public schools, but are not as relaxed as in alternative schools. Often, students have to compete against students throughout their area to get into magnet schools. People in magnet schools are usually highly motivated, carry a high point grade average and/or have special talents. If you think this is for you, talk to your counselor to see what your chances are.

You may decide to go to a private school. Rules at private schools are often tougher or easier than the rules in public schools. Whether you find things tougher or easier at a private school will depend on which one you choose.

To help you decide, you and your parents should visit several private schools before you make up your mind. Talk to the administrators; ask to visit classes while they are in session. Do the teachers sound like they know what they are talking about? Do the kids seem to be well behaved or are they acting up and disrupting the class?

Does the school have up-to-date equipment? Is there a computer lab? How about a science lab? Is there a workshop? If you hate Shop, that will not matter. But if you want to take Shop, you should find a school that has shop equipment and a qualified shop teacher.

Parochial schools are private schools run by religious groups, and some of your classes will include religious teachings. If you decide to go to a parochial school, you and your parents should visit the school and look for the things mentioned for private schools.

When you consider going to a private school, whether it is a secular or parochial school, you have to consider how much you will have to pay. Some schools give scholarships. Some give tuition credit if parents donate time at the school. Some offer other forms of assistance. But some do not do any of these things. So private schools are sometimes luxuries instead of necessities.

Another way to get an education is to study at home. Studying at home was the way most kids learned before the government decided kids should study in a building called a school. During the early years, most of those schools were one-room schoolhouses. All students sat in one room and one teacher taught them. If you were going to school then, you would probably have a kindergartner in the seat next to you.

Not all parents wanted their children to go to school, and some taught their children at home until the militia marched the children to school and made sure they went every day. The law still makes sure you go to school, but now, in some cases, you can go to school at home.

In 1972, the U.S. Supreme Court decided home schooling was legal, and it is now legal in every state. But some states put restrictions on "home" schools. Some insist the person who teaches has to be certified by the state. Other states insist the home has to be registered as a private school. Whatever the requirements, if you want to be taught at home and your parents want to teach you, you can legally reach your career goals without leaving your house.

Before you make a decision, think about what not leaving your house in the morning will mean. You will not be with kids your own age. Not being with kids your own age may not present a problem if you have friends you can hang out with after they get out of traditional school for the day or on

the weekends and during summer vacation. If you belong to clubs where you can be with young people, that may be enough contact for you. You have to make that decision.

Something else you should consider is that you will be with your parents all day. If your parents are always on your case, being with them all day instead of being in a traditional school may be more than you can handle. But if you do not have a problem spending big pockets of time with your parents, home schooling is a way of getting an education that can help you reach your goals.

TAKE CONTROL OF YOUR CLASSES

Before you charge into your classes and start ordering kids and the teachers around, read on!

By the time you graduate from high school, you will have spent more than 10,000 hours in school. It may seem to you that you were bored during every one of those hours. But if you think back, you will remember the time you hit a home run and won the game for your sixth grade team. Then there was the time the best looking girl in your science class smiled at you. And how about the time you thought you failed a test and you came up with a B? Those were exciting moments.

But it is fair to say a lot of your time in school is boring. Everything in life is boring some of the time. You have spent a lot of boring hours watching television or at the mall or at parties. No way, you say. You love television. You love cruising the mall. And parties are the greatest. Be honest.

How many times have you walked away from the television set because what was on bored you? How about the time you had to take your eight-year-old visiting cousin to the mall? It is hard to flirt while you have an eight-year-old kid yelling about wanting to go into the toy store. And what

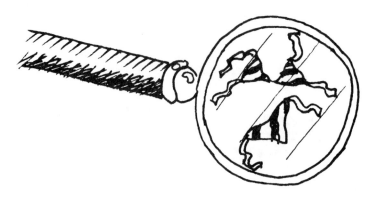

about the party your best friend gave? Her parents did not leave the room all evening. Every time you tried to dance close to a guy, they gave you the kind of look your parents gave you when you came home with a bathing suit that could fit in the palm of your hand.

Life is not always exciting or interesting. But it should not always be dull and boring.

WHY CLASSES ARE SOMETIMES BORING

Some of your classes may be boring because you are not interested in what you have to learn, because the teacher does not explain things so you can understand them, or because you already know the stuff she is teaching. For instance, if your parents drilled you almost every day on multiplication tables since third grade, you will not get excited about reviews of multiplication tables.

There are different reasons why you are bored in school. Maybe it is just a boring day for you or a boring week. But if you are constantly bored, start figuring out ways to jazz up your life. Inheriting a million dollars and quitting school may jazz you, but that is not going to happen, so be realistic.

If your classes totally gross you out, you can try to change the things you hate most about them. Whether you succeed or not will depend on how much the people who run the school will listen to you.

> "Repetition, repetition, repetition. That's all I get. How many times do I have to learn where China is? Who cares?"

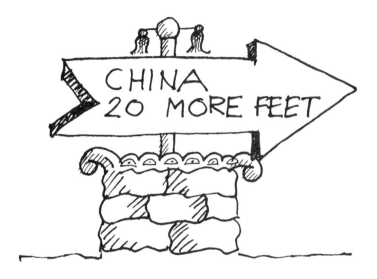

If the administrators and teachers at your school believe the best way to teach is to teach the way classes have been taught for years, you will have to work hard to get them to accept change. These people usually stay with lesson plans and seldom, if ever, break the rules. They think the way to teach is to give information, repeat the information, and have you repeat it in class and at home by doing homework. These teachers teach with very little class participation or discussion.

On the other hand, if your administrators and teachers believe one teaching method does not work for everybody, you have a better chance of making changes. These people have lesson plans, but they are willing to make changes which make learning more interesting. These teachers ask questions and encourage students to ask questions. This makes learning a two-way street instead of a dead end.

For years, some teachers have tried to find a perfect way to teach. There is no perfect way. All they can do is try to help as many students as they can. The problem is that not everybody learns at the same pace. Some catch onto things fast, some take more time to catch on, and some often do not catch on at all. Because there are usually more kids in the middle category than there are in the others, teachers often aim their teaching at the kids in the middle—the ones who take time to catch on but who do catch on. This leaves the others bored, angry, or both.

So what can you do to make life more interesting in school? Just trying to make changes will make your life more interesting. Sometimes people are bored because they are not challenged. Making changes will give you challenges. And once you get going, you may find you are the kind of person who can get kids to do things that will make their lives better. The more kids you have with you, the better chance you will have of making changes in your school.

Start by making a list. Draw a line down the center of a paper. On the left side of the line, write everything you like about your school. On the right side write everything you do not like. If this has been a bad day for you, the right side will be longer than the left side. Even if it has been a good day, the right side may be longer than the left side. People often think negative. So keep the list handy to add more positive things before you present your list. It is important to have the positive list longer than the negative list.

You will not get administrators and teachers to listen to you if you show them a list with thirty-five things you do not like about the school and only one or two that you do like. So go over the list and start taking things out of the negative side. Decide what you want the most. Do you want to work independently on a special project? Do you want to work ahead of the other kids because you already know what they are learning? Do you want less homework, especially "papers"? Why should you have to write a ten-page paper about aard-varks unless you are into African pigs?

After you bring your list down to three or four negative things, list them in order of their importance to you. Then choose the administrator or teacher you think will be willing to listen to your ideas. Pick a time when the person you choose will not be rushing off to teach a class or to have lunch. Be ready to give reasons why you want to make changes. Making changes because you are bored will not win you a lot of points. Making changes to better prepare yourself for college or for a job probably will.

✈ MAKING SCHOOL MORE INTERESTING

If you get all the changes you ask for, say thank you and celebrate. If you get only one of the things you want, say thank you and celebrate even though you did not get everything. If you do not get anything, say thank you and celebrate for having the courage to try.

A strikeout does not mean total defeat although it may seem like it is. Try again with the same demands but with a different approach, or try new demands. If you keep striking out and things stay pretty much the way they have been since you started high school, take control of the part of your school life you can control.

Although there are certain classes you have to take before you get your high school diploma, you may not have to sit in classes all day wishing you were someplace else. Try to get permission from your parents and teachers to skip a grade. Or you can work ahead. Or if you already know what is being taught in a class, ask to "test out." This means you can take a test on the subject, and if you pass the test, you will be out of the class. Then you can take one that is more challenging, interesting, or just plain fun.

Check out the elective classes your school offers and take the ones that will help you reach your goals. Take advanced placement courses. AP classes are challenging, and you can earn credits toward your college degree.

Although there are AP classes in almost every subject, your school may have only a few, and you may have to settle for French instead of Russian. Or you may have to choose English Literature instead of Creative Writing. But chances are you will not be bored.

If your school does not offer AP courses, ask your counselor if there is a school nearby where you can take the courses. If there is not, you may be able to take a test in the different subjects without taking the courses. If you pass, you will get college credits in those subjects. There is a charge to take the tests, but the fee is less than college tuition.

If AP classes are not challenging enough for you

and you "test out" of enough classes, you may be able to go to high school part time while you take college courses at a local college.

This schedule will challenge you and will let you graduate with your friends.

Although AP classes should be at the top of your elective class list if you plan to go to college, you will still have other elective classes to choose from. Do not take them only because you need the credits to graduate. Choose elective classes because you are interested in the subject or because you enjoy them. Keep in mind that high school does not have to be endless days of total misery.

🐾 DON'T JUDGE A CLASS BY ITS NAME

Classes named Science and Mathematics probably scare you. A two-hour session in the dentist's chair may be more welcomed than fifty minutes in science or math. And besides, why do you need them? You have no ambition to build the world's most sophisticated robot. You just want to be able to troubleshoot your computer when it seems to have a mind of its own.

Learning to solve scientific and mathematical problems through trial and error can help you become the best rocket scientist in the universe, or it can help you prove to your computer that you are the boss. The scientific and mathematical skills you learn in science and math classes can also help you solve everyday situations throughout your life. And the skills can be used to learn how to build a house, fix your car, or make chocolate fudge.

Social Studies include history, geography, economics, and political science. These come together to teach you about the world, past and present, and how economics and politics have affected it and may affect it. In your social studies classes you will learn about different forms of government. Why were they created? Why are thousands of people dying of hunger? How can injustices be corrected?

Learning about the past teaches you where you came from. Why did your ancestors leave their country to come to a new one? Why was your grandfather a farmer? Was that the only way he could feed his family, or was he a farmer because he loved the land?

How many languages do you speak? If you speak only one, do not miss the opportunity to learn another. Most high schools require that you take at least one foreign language to earn your diploma. Even if a foreign language is not required, take one anyway. You will learn about another country and another culture. And languages help you communicate whether that communication is with the boy who lives across the street or with your cousin across the world. Knowing a second language may even help you get a job. Employers often hire people who speak more than one language before they hire people who speak only one.

Take typing and computer classes. Knowing how to touch-type and how to use a computer will be useful in college and throughout your life. These skills are also a plus when you apply for certain kinds of jobs.

Art and Music may seem like easy ways to earn credits toward your diploma, but these can be more than easy credits. Art and music will be part of your life whether you create it, experience it, or both. You can enjoy fine art and music while you are alone or while you are surrounded by people.

And the skills you learn during these classes could lead to career opportunities.

Industrial Arts can prepare you for a career and give you life skills such as engine repair, printing, woodworking, and home repair.

Physical Education makes your body stronger and your mind sharper. After all the sitting your body does, it needs exercise and PE gives it to you. Physical Education also teaches you how to play sports and how to be a good sport, a skill that will help you in your personal and professional life.

USE CLASSES TO YOUR ADVANTAGE

Whether you plan to go to college or not, some of the classes offered by your school will help you prepare for a career. For instance, there may be classes that can start you on a medical career. What? You be a doctor or a nurse? Maybe, maybe not. It could happen. But you do not have to be a doctor or a nurse to be part of the medical field.

You can be a medical secretary or a medical records clerk. You can be a hospital admitting clerk or a medical transcriber. There are even jobs for medical artists to draw pictures for medical books. So if you like the field of medicine and you like to draw, why not combine the two? Take art classes in high school to perfect your drawing skills, and take science classes to learn about the human body.

Maybe you do not like the medical field. Maybe anything that has to do with medicine gives you the shakes. You can use your drawing skills in other areas such as technical illustration. Technical illustrators usually make three-dimensional drawings in pencil, ink, oil, watercolors, or anything that creates eye-catching illustrations for newspapers, catalogues, and sometimes for books and music albums.

Maybe you are always trying new hairdos and makeup. Maybe people ask you to fix their hair or their makeup. If you like doing these things, check to see if your school has classes that will teach you how to become a beautician. If there are none, ask your counselor if there is a school where you can take a cosmetology course for high school credit.

If cosmetology is not for you, there are a lot of different things you can do with your life. Ask your counselor if you can take elective classes at other schools. If you live in a small city, you may not have many choices. But if you live in a large city, you may have more choices than you need.

Some schools let their students take off-campus elective high school classes for office careers, auto body repair, welding, banking, computers, brick masonry, and some things you probably have not thought of yet. Your counselor can tell you what is available and can help you make decisions about what classes to take. His job is to help you, so do not be nervous about talking to him.

Some counselors only see students by appointment. Some are more relaxed about schedules. Find out what the rules are at your school, then go along with them. When you talk to the counselor, be polite and have questions ready. And ask about pamphlets. Counselors often have pamphlets about college information, trade schools, job opportunities, and the Reserve Officer Training Corps (ROTC).

Your counselor can also help if you have trouble staying in school because of low grades or money problems. Some schools have tutoring programs to help you catch up on some of your classes, to help you understand what you read, and to help you pass tests so you can get your diploma. If you missed classes because of illness or because of personal problems that kept you from going to school, ask your counselor about "open-entry" classes. These let you go into a class at any time and let you quit as soon as you catch up to your regular studies.

"I want to stay in school but I have to quit. My family needs money to pay the rent."

If you are faced with having to quit school because you have to help support yourself or your family, ask if your school has a school-work program. Some high schools have longer class days than others to help students like you. If you cannot go to all your classes during regular hours, you may be able to go as early as eight or as late as six and take some classes on Saturdays.

These arrangements are often part of a Dropout Prevention and Recovery Program. This program has Skill Centers to help you train for a career and to help you get self-confidence in your studies and in your life. Some of the skills offered are electronics, refrigeration/air conditioning, cable TV installer, filing clerk, and receptionist. Ask your counselor to help you.

Some schools are so small, the counselor may

be a teacher. Whoever your counselor is, do not quit school without talking to him. A high school diploma puts the odds on your side. High school graduates often get better jobs and feel better about themselves than kids who do not have a diploma.

IV
COLLEGE IS NOT FOR EVERYONE

Some kids go to high school because the law says they have to go until they reach a certain age. Some go because they think school is easier than working. Some go because they believe education will help them get a better job.

Whatever your reason for being in high school, learn something. Those words will sound weird to people who go to school to learn. But if you hang out with kids whose main reason for being in school is so they will not have to go to work, it does not sound weird. To these kids fun is top priority.

One girl took a computer class so she could be with her boyfriend. By the end of the semester she was so hooked on how computers worked, she took another computer class to sharpen her skills even though her boyfriend wanted her to take history with him. When the girl was old enough to legally quit school, she stayed, got her diploma, and worked part-time to pay for classes to learn how to repair computers.

So, as long as you are in school, learn something even if that something is nothing more than that you have choices in life. With luck, you may find out what your choice is at this time in your life. You may also realize what you decide at six-teen, eighteen, or twenty does not lock you in for-ever. Life has *off* ramps. Which off ramp you choose can give you a happier, healthier life.

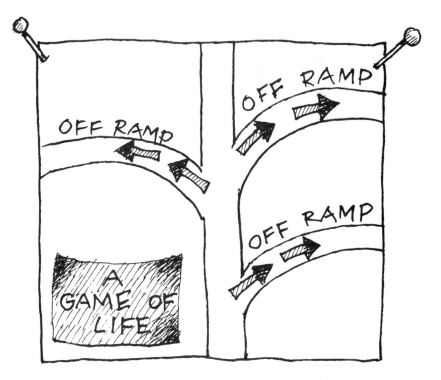

Friends, parents, and teachers can help you make choices. Your school guidance counselor can too. This person has information about how to join the armed forces, how to get on-the-job training, how to get into trade and vocational schools, how to apply for college, and how to get money for col-lege.

Even if your choice is to quit school as soon as you are old enough to legally quit, talk to your counselor. Whether you are quitting because you hate school, or you have to go to work because your family needs money to eat and pay the rent, or you have messed around so much your grades are lower than a snake's belly, see a counselor before you make the final decision. There may be an off ramp you do not know about.

✺ HIGH SCHOOL DIPLOMAS

"Why do I need a high school diploma? It's just a piece of paper."

Many years ago, people with high school diplomas were often considered well educated. If you had been looking for a job then, your chances of getting work after you graduated from high school were better than they are today. Maybe the job would not be the kind of work you wanted, but you probably would have earned more money than the millions of people without high school diplomas.

In today's market, a high school diploma still often gets you a higher paying job than people who do not have their diplomas. But the money you earn will usually be less than people who continue their education get. So unless you have a rich relative who will make you president of his company the day you graduate from high school, you may want to continue your education after graduation.

One way of doing this is to join the armed forces. Many men and women have joined the air force, army, marines, navy, or coast guard right out of high school. You may decide to make the military your career, or you may stay in only a few years. But during those years, you can get training in many professions.

If you stay a civilian, you may be able to continue your education with on-the-job training. In other words, you train while you are on the job. The boss considers you such a hard worker and so eager to learn that he teaches you more and more about his business. He promotes you often and gives you raises. This does not happen to goof-offs. Often it does not even happen to people who work hard. But it does happen.

One boy was hired a week after graduation to help a man deliver furniture. The boy worked so hard the driver hired him full time and taught him how to carry the furniture so it would not get broken or scratched. He showed him how to talk to customers and handle the paperwork. Eventually, the man let the boy drive the truck. When business grew, the driver bought a bigger truck and let the boy drive the smaller one.

Another way to get on-the-job training is to start your own business. But without practical or business skills, your chances of succeeding are small. If the business fails, you will be back where you started—unemployed. If the business succeeds, you will find there are so many things you do not know about running a business, you will probably go back to school to learn how to make your company more efficient and more successful.

TRADE AND VOCATIONAL SCHOOLS

These schools teach courses that will help you develop your skills. But before you apply, you should ask yourself what you like to do. Keep in mind, you will probably spend eight hours a day, five days a week, working at your job. You will be happier and more successful if you like your work. Whatever you decide, you will find there are a lot of people ready to help you reach your goal.

There are schools that will teach you how to become an actor, secretary, computer operator, medical or dental technician, carpenter, almost anything you want.

You may have heard commercials for these schools on television or seen their ads in magazines and newspapers. If you live in a large city, you will find many of the schools listed in the business pages of your phone book. If you live in a small city where there are few or no schools listed, you will find books in the library that give names of schools and their addresses. Ask the librarian for help. If you cannot travel to a school to study, some schools will teach you by mail through their correspondence courses.

➤ CHOOSE CAREFULLY

There are laws to protect you from being cheated when you register at one of these schools. Many people who run them are honest. But there is a saying in business that has been around for a long time. Buyer beware. Keep this motto in mind whether you are buying clothes, a stereo, a car, or putting out a bunch of money for classes.

Never let yourself get pressured into signing an enrollment contract. Recruiters often get paid according to the number of students they sign up. So you may be given a sales pitch that will make a used car salesman sound like an amateur. No matter how excited you are about the promises the recruiter makes, do not sign on the spot.

Take the contract home and check the small print. The letters and the numbers may be tiny and the lines close together. This will make the contract hard to read. But read every word to make sure there are no terms that you do not agree with.

If the contract is too hard for you to understand, ask somebody to check it over. When you sign a contract, you are responsible for everything in it.

Ask the school recruiter for names of students who graduated from the school and of students who are still studying there. Ask if you can talk to them. If the recruiter will not give you any names, hang around after classes and talk to students as they come out of classes. Ask them if they are satisfied with the things they are learning. Ask them if the teachers know what they are talking about.

Also, ask business owners about the school. If you want to learn about hairdressing, ask beauty salon owners to suggest a school. Talk to employers. Employers sometimes hire their workers from professional schools. If the school you are thinking of going to does not train students well, these people will know.

Ask the school recruiter if you can look at the textbooks, the classrooms, and the equipment. Ask about financial aid programs. Ask if you can get a partial refund if you do not finish the course. Ask about the dropout rate, job placement, and starting salaries of the school's graduates. If the recruiter answers these questions, thank him. If he does not, tell him the law says an applicant has to be given this information.

Ask if the school is licensed. The government gives a license to a school if it proves it has enough money to run the school properly. The school also has to prove the teachers are well trained; the curriculum is strong; and the students are motivated to study and to succeed in their chosen profession. If the school is not licensed, look for a different school.

If you are checking out schools while you are still in high school, your counselor can help you. If you do not want to talk to your counselor, ask a teacher, parents, or other relatives. If you do not like talking to them, find somebody you feel you can trust with your future.

One boy, who was working as a dishwasher in a fancy restaurant, trusted the chef. There are schools that teach people how to become chefs. But this boy did not have to go to school to learn. As the weeks and months passed and the chef saw how hard the boy worked and how interested he was in the art of cooking, the chef gave him more and more responsibility. Eventually, the boy opened his own restaurant.

While this boy was in high school, he thought he would work as a laborer all his life, like his mother and father. Now, he makes enough money to take care of them. They did not go beyond third grade. He graduated from high school. Now his daughter goes to college.

"Education is a miraculous thing," he says.

TIME WAITS FOR NO ONE

It is hard to find enough time to survive high school. Your parents say, "Clean your room." Your girlfriend says, "Let's go to the beach." Your boyfriend says, "Let's go to the mall." Your friends say, "Let's go to the concert." Your teacher says, "Your twenty-five-page paper on the cure for acne is due in two days." If you knew the cure for acne, you would bottle the formula and make a fortune. You would never have to worry about money again. But you would still have to worry about time.

Money can buy a lot of things. But, no matter how much money you have or how smart you are, you cannot buy extra hours. Everybody—rich, poor, young, old—gets twenty-four hours every day, seven days every week, 365 days every year, except during leap year when everybody gets an extra day at the end of February. But not everybody uses time the same way. You have seen people who are always trying to catch up. You have seen some who always seem to have everything done, plus time to relax. The way you use time will make surviving high school harder or easier.

⚡ MAKING TIME WORK FOR YOU

Before you can make your life easier, you may have to lose some time. Not a lot. Just enough to make a schedule. If you are already short on time, where will you find more to make a schedule? You can do it with pockets of time.

Try to think of ways to save time while you are getting dressed, walking to school, eating, or doing chores. Maybe you can cut a few minutes off your shower. Or your phone time. Or your television watching. Or off the time you spend at the mall.

Other pockets of time happen when you are waiting. People wait a lot. You wait to talk to the teacher, the counselor, the nurse, the school secretary. You wait to pay for something you bought at the mall; you wait to renew your driver's license; you wait to buy lunch at your favorite fast-food place. You do not always have paper and pen ready to write a schedule, but keep thinking about it. Then when you sit down to write how to manage your time, your brain will spit out the information.

So how do you begin your schedule? Begin by subtracting hours from the twenty-four hours you have every day. Take away eight hours for sleep. Many people do not get an eight-hour block of sleep every day. They get more. They get less. They take naps, or they crash over weekends to try to catch up. Whatever your sleeping pattern is, chances are you will have about sixteen hours to do other things every day.

Other things include eating. Eating can take a lot of time when you eat with your family. Or it can take less time if you eat with your friends or alone. It takes even less time from your sixteen hours if you eat while you do other things. This is not the healthiest way to eat, but it saves time. Sometimes you may have to do it.

Something else you have to do is go to classes. How many hours do you spend in classes? This does not mean how many days you show up. It means how many classes you have to pass to graduate. Then there is homework. How many hours do you spend on homework? How many hours should you spend on it to get passing grades? How many hours should you spend on it to get the grades you will need to get into a good college? If you are thinking one hour, think again. Three or four is closer to reality.

There may be other things in your life you absolutely have to do that other kids do not have to do. The key word is "absolutely." If the word fits, add the time spent on these things to the hours you spend sleeping, eating, going to classes, and doing homework. Subtract this number from the twenty-four hours everybody has every day. The answer is the number of hours you have left in your day to do other things.

How are you doing? Have you run out of hours yet? Probably not if you add the days when you are not in school, or you do not have homework. If you are still short of hours, you have to adjust, readjust, and eliminate.

If you are part of every activity and every club in school, start eliminating some. Do not go to the extreme and quit everything. You need these for personal growth, friends, and fun. And if you plan to go to college, remember that people who make decisions on your application will give your extra-curricular activities serious consideration. But they consider some more than others.

They are not wild about rock fan clubs, Roller Coaster Riders Club or similar activities. They are wild about student government, community service and varsity sports, among others. But do not give up something you really enjoy for something you hate. You will be miserable and your schedule will suffer.

If you are working, you have to deduct the number of hours you work from the time you have left of your twenty-four. This may be where you can do some adjusting. You can quit the job. But work experience is something college admissions people look at when they study your application.

If you cannot quit your job because your family needs the money, or you need it to buy clothes, or a car, or go out to have fun and relax, there is help. Many schools have programs where students can earn class credits while working. Regulations vary. But most schools have schedules that allow you to earn work experience credits every semester.

The job must be acceptable to your counselor, and there must be adult supervision while you are working. You must have a work permit, and you must sign an agreement that you will follow the work experience rules. Ask your counselor what the rules are in your school. Despite the regulations, work experience education is an excellent way to save time.

Keep reworking your schedule. By doing this, you will not overcommit yourself. Maybe a weekly schedule will work better for you than a daily schedule. Maybe you need a monthly one. Choose the schedule that works best for you. Overcommitment often leads to stress.

❧ HANDLING STRESS

There is enough stress in your life without adding to it by promising to do more than you can do. So think before you say you will head the committee to hold a frog jumping contest. Or that you will spend the weekend passing out flyers to warn people spaceships will land in their city on the Fourth of July. The word "no" is a perfectly good word. Use it and you will cut down on stress.

Stress usually comes when you have more things loaded on you than your mind and body can handle. The experiences can be emotional or physical or both. These include moving to a a new area, the loss of a friend, or a divorce in your family. Or it can be happy, exciting moments like getting your first car, going out on your first date, or winning the lottery.

Do not be surprised if starting high school causes stress. High school means a change in your life. And changes often cause stress. But change is not always bad. Without change you would never grow emotionally and intellectually. How would you like to be the same person at eighteen that you were at eight? Boring!

There is good stress and bad stress. The good stress gives you survival instincts. It kicks in when you are in physical danger or you think you are. This kind of stress is called *fight or flight*, and it prepares your body to handle an immediate problem or danger.

For thousands of years, animals and people have been programmed to act when they are threatened. One way to act is to fight. Another way is to run away. Watch animals when they meet. Unless they are used to being together, their bodies stiffen, they may circle each other, or go into a fighting pose. Watch kids in the hall. One bumps into the other and starts pushing. They glare. Bodies stiffen.

Suppose you are cornered in the bathroom by the girl who tripped you on purpose in gym. You are still limping from the fall and there she is hovering over you. Your heart beats quicker than the drummer in the school band. Your muscles tense.

In each example, the body has become prepared to defend itself or run away.

Your body reacts to stress all the time. It may be the way you get through your biology test. Or the way you kick a field goal with time running out on the clock. Without fight or flight, your body might not have the spurt of energy to help you protect yourself, learn endless information, or accept new adventures.

So do not try to get rid of stress entirely. You cannot anyway and trying to get rid of it will just create more stress. Besides, the only way you can get stress out of your life is to vegetate. This may

help you reach your goal of being stress free, but vegetating will also keep you from reaching your other goals!

A big part of stress is feeling out of control. So learn to handle stress by not overloading your day. Making time work for you will give you control. Like any machine, your body has limits. The longer you stay in the fight or flight mode, the more your body is likely to break down. This can make you depressed or give you headaches, backaches, rashes, and other problems. Getting rid of fears reduces stress. What scares you the most? Whatever it is, ask yourself why this thing scares you. Try to figure out a way to stop being afraid or to make yourself less afraid. Bad grades that lead to failure usually scare high school students the most.

One boy said, "The whole time I've been in school, I've been called gifted. This dominates everything I do. If I fail a class, I'll have nothing to live for." A girl said, "I'm afraid of getting bad grades. No matter how much I tell people I don't care what grades I get, I do care. I have trouble sleeping and I can't eat when I have a test coming up."

The boy has been in the fight or flight stress a long time and is in physical and emotional trouble. He is seeing a therapist to help him deal with the problem. The girl is in better shape. Although she has trouble sleeping and eating before a test, she does great on pop quizzes. When a teacher slips one of these on her, the fight stress comes to her help. It puts her brain in high gear and she aces the quiz. This makes her feel more positive about herself and lessens her stress.

Other comments about fear from high school students: "I'm afraid of the opposite sex." "Of being trashed by seniors." "Of loneliness." "I'm not afraid of nothing." "I'm afraid dragons are not real."

The first three situations definitely create stress. The boy who said he was not afraid of "nothing" probably is afraid of many things, which creates stress. The girl who said she was afraid dragons were not real was probably the least stressed person in the group on that particular day. The next day may be different.

When you feel slightly stressed, you may feel better after taking a few deep breaths and then going on with what you were doing. Exercise also lessens stress. Running and swimming are great for your body and your mind. During strenuous exercise your brain generates *endorphins* which can give you a natural "high" that usually makes you feel better about yourself.

Relaxing is a great way to reduce stress. But some people get more stressed when they try it because they do not know how to relax. One way to overcome the problem is to sit down, close your eyes, then think about your muscles. Start with your feet and your legs, go to your stomach, your upper body, and finally to your head. Tense and then relax each area. While you are doing this, breathe through your nose and concentrate on the rhythm of your tensing and breathing.

Do it at least fifteen minutes, then sit quietly for several minutes before you go on to something else. Do not be disappointed if you are not as relaxed as you would like to be. The relaxation method takes practice.

Stress does not come on schedule. You are probably more stressed after reading about stress than you were before you started. But now you know ways to reduce stress. Try the method you think will work best for you. Your body will thank you!

HEALTH AND HAZARDS

To survive high school, you have to eat, drink liquids, and get some sleep. This does not mean staying up half the night, drinking gallons of soda, or stuffing your mouth with junk food all the time. It means getting enough sleep, drinking a lot of water, and eating foods that keep your body well and strong.

Many people take better care of their cars than they take care of their bodies. They put the best gas in the tank so the car can run. They make sure there is oil in the engine so it will hum. They give the radiator water, so it will not overheat. And they do not drive the car nonstop until it wears out. Think of your body as a car. Give it what it needs.

STAYING HEALTHY

Not everybody needs the same amount of sleep to function well in school. But it is generally recognized by experts that eight hours of sleep a night is average for most people. If you do not fall asleep in class with only seven hours of sleep for five or six nights, or if after eight hours of sleep every night for a week, you feel tired, you may not be an "average" sleeper. So find out how much sleep you need to feel your best and try to get that amount every night.

There will be times when you will sleep fewer hours than you need, without problems. There are kids to talk to on the phone, TV to watch, parties to go to, sports to play, tests to study for, personal problems to worry about or solve. But if you miss a lot of sleep over a long period of time, your body will rebel. It will not function the way you want it to function. It may even decide to make you sick so you can get the rest you need. Being sick may not bother you if it keeps you home from school. But being sick will mess up your social life if you cannot go to the big dance.

Next to air, water is the most important ingredient your body needs. In fact, water is so important, healthy people have survived for two months without food. But the body cannot live more than a week without water.

Yet, many people drink water only when there are no other liquids around. But other liquids, especially sodas and beer, cannot take the place of water. In fact, they work against your body. They drain liquids from your system, including some of the water your body stored to stay well.

Doctors say you should drink eight cups of water a day. To get that much water, do not wait until you are thirsty to drink. Whenever you pass a water fountain, take a drink. Take a big one. Water works with the food you eat to give you energy.

To help you keep your energy high and your mind alert, you need to eat food from different food groups.

Breads, grains, and cereals give your body energy and help your brain work. If you are not eating enough of this group, you will feel tired and may not be quick enough to come up with an answer when the teacher asks you a question.

Meat, fish, and beans give you protein. These help your body grow, your hair shine, and your nails stay strong so they will not break every time you open your notebook.

Milk and cheese give you calcium. These make your bones and teeth strong.

Fruits and vegetables give you lots of vitamins, especially vitamins A and C which keep your gums and skin in good shape.

High school is a time when your body is still growing, and your bones are still forming. If you want your bones strong enough to hold up your developing body, and you are not eating these foods, you may have to change your diet.

This does not mean you have to give up hot dogs, hamburgers, and french fries. But it does mean you have to cut down on these fatty foods and change your diet so you will get a variety of foods. By varying the kinds of foods you eat, you will supply your body with the nutrients it needs to stay healthy.

The care you give your body while it is developing into adulthood may be the key to your health later in life. If you develop healthy habits now, you will probably keep those habits throughout your life.

❧ EATING DISORDERS

To some people, eating is more than something they do every day. To these people, food becomes a way of life which can develop into eating disorders known as anorexia or bulimia. Although males have eating disorders, most people who have anorexia nervosa or bulimia nervosa are females. The problem appears when they enter their teens, when they start high school, or sometimes, when they are graduating or making plans to leave home.

Anorexia means absence of appetite. But most people with anorexia do not lose their appetites. They actually feel hungry almost all the time, but hardly eat. A common term for the condition is *starver* because people with this problem starve themselves.

Kids need super doses of acceptance, understanding, and attention. Many do not think they get enough of these. Some handle the problem by talking to their friends, parents, teachers, or to other people they trust. Others rebel against authority by taking drugs or drinking too much. Some starve.

"Thin is beautiful and I'm going to be the most beautiful girl in school."

Since many girls think thin is beautiful, they diet when they see their bodies getting rounder and more mature during puberty. But most stop within days or weeks. They may diet again but then stop again. The kids, girls or boys, who constantly diet are the ones who are most likely to develop eating disorders.

An anorexic goes way beyond dieting. She believes being thin, thin, thin will make people notice her, and she is right. When she goes from 120 pounds to 80 pounds, people cannot help but notice. Although she gets the attention she longs for, it is the wrong kind of attention. Nobody says she is beautifully thin. How can they without lying?

A person who is in an advanced stage of anorexia looks sick. She has little energy. Her hair is dull. Her skin is dry. Her lips and fingers may have a bluish look. This is what people can see. What they cannot see is that the lack of proper nutrition is ruining her internal organs. Ruining her body was not what the anorexic had in mind. All she wanted to do was be thinner so people would think she was beautiful.

But once the starving pattern is set, it is hard to stop. Anorexics need help from their family, friends, and most of the time, they need therapy to stop the destructive actions.

Bulimarexia and bulimia nervosa are the correct words for the condition that causes people to binge eat and then make themselves vomit. But many people call them *bingers*. Whatever name is used, bingers are people who eat large amounts of food and then make themselves throw up. Some doctors believe bingers were starvers before they became bingers.

Bingers have basically the same problems as starvers, and looking beautiful is at the top of their list. They usually believe their weight is making them ugly. So, although they put food in their mouth, when they finish eating, they usually make themselves throw up.

At first, the binger has to put a finger or two down her throat to help her get rid of the food. But after a while, the vomiting becomes easier. Eventually, all she has to do is stand over the toilet and tense her muscles. After a while, she may not be able to control the vomiting.

Binging and purging mess up the body. The brain and kidneys are damaged by potassium loss and dehydration. Because teeth are exposed to stomach acid, they can be harmed. The acid also irritates the esophagus and can cause damage.

Some people cannot make themselves vomit, so they overuse laxatives and some use substances that make them vomit. The overuse of these substances and of laxatives can kill without warning.

Although starvers and bingers have things in common, one of the differences is that bingers can hide their problem more easily than starvers. The starver looks like a skeleton. Bingers may look just a bit underweight and can hide their destructive actions for longer periods of time. But starvers and bingers are heading in the same dangerous direction.

🐺 SMOKES, BOOZE, AND OTHER DRUGS

If you think about something often during the day, if you feel you cannot live without what you focus on, or your body is uncomfortable without it, you are addicted. When a person's life centers around something above everything else, that person is an addict.

You can be addicted to compulsive eating, chocolate, caffeine, shopping, sports, gambling, tobacco, alcohol, drugs, anything that controls your life. The addictions that affect young people the most are drugs.

Many people do not think of tobacco and alcohol as drugs. But they are "legal" drugs. This does not mean it is safe to use them. It means it is legal to buy them if you are considered old enough under the law.

Tobacco, whether you smoke it or chew it, causes cancer and heart disease. These illnesses probably will not kill you while you are in high school. But if you continue to use tobacco, your chances of dying from cancer or heart disease are much higher than they are in people who have never used tobacco or have stopped using it.

Because smoking affects your lungs, tobacco will also make it harder to play sports. To race down the court for the winning basket or to run ninety yards (82.30 m) for a touchdown, you need healthy lungs. Without them, you may not make it past the fifty-yard line. Smoking also causes yellow teeth, bad breath, and a dry cough which are not pleasant to your kissing partner!

⇒ ALCOHOL

It is against the law for minors to use alcohol. And it is against the law for anyone to sell it to them. The age when a person can legally buy or drink alcohol varies from state to state.

Despite the fact that drinking alcohol is illegal, kids drink it because "everybody's doing it" and they want to be part of the crowd. Some drink because they do not feel good about themselves. Some kids do it because they are shy and the alcohol makes them more talkative. Most of the time being more talkative makes them sound like idiots.

If you want to help a friend who thinks liquor

makes him fit in with the popular kids on campus, tape him while he is drunk, then let him hear the tape when he is sober. It may not keep him from drinking again, but it will show him how stupid alcohol makes him sound.

Young people get more drunk on less alcohol and stay drunk longer on the smaller amount than adults. This is because young people's bodies are still immature which makes them absorb alcohol faster than adult bodies.

The moment you take a drink, the liquor affects every organ in your body. The more you drink, the more damage the alcohol causes. It affects brain cells, eats up the linings of your stomach and your intestines, and deteriorates your heart muscles. This does not happen in a week, a day, or a month. But the earlier you begin drinking, the greater your chance of an early death from alcoholism.

Too much alcohol can stunt your emotional, physical, and intellectual growth. Alcohol also affects unborn babies. Women who drink while they are pregnant may have smaller babies. And these babies will probably be less healthy than babies whose mothers do not drink while pregnant.

There is no cure for alcoholism. The only way to stop the disease from destroying your body is to stop drinking. Alcoholics who stop drinking totally are called *recovering alcoholics*. Most reached the recovery stage with help from Alcoholics Anonymous (AA). This organization has helped millions recover from alcohol, and there are AA groups all over the world. If you think your drinking is out of control, look up the Alcoholics Anonymous number in the phone book, or ask your telephone operator for the number.

How can you tell if your drinking is out of control? If you are wondering about it, your drinking is probably out of control, or you are getting close to being out of control. If you tried to cut down or stop, but have not been able to, if you say you will drink only on weekends and you crave a drink on Tuesday during algebra, if you want a drink when a teacher yells at you or a kid shoves you in the lunch line, your drinking is controlling you instead of you controlling your drinking.

So if you do not use alcohol, do not start. One way not to start is to stay away from kids who use it. If you do drink, do not drive. Drunk driving accidents are the number one killer of teenagers.

One mother raced to the police station after getting a call saying her sixteen-year-old son had been arrested for driving while drunk, running a red light, and crippling a man. The mother told the officer she did not know her son drank liquor. Then she added how relieved she was that her son was not on drugs. The officer told her alcohol was a drug as deadly as cocaine and heroin. The difference was that alcohol was legal. In this accident, the teenager did not die. But he went to prison. The man he crippled died from injuries a week after the accident, and the boy was convicted of vehicular manslaughter.

ILLEGAL DRUGS

Marijuana, also called pot or grass, can damage your immune system. This makes you more susceptible to diseases. It can damage your lungs, raise your blood pressure, produce memory loss, interfere with coordination, impair your speech and vision, and cause mood changes. You may have heard some or all of this is not true. But tests show these things can happen to your body if you use marijuana.

77

All drugs are bad for your body. But some are more deadly than others.

"Come on. A few hits of crack will pick you up for the test."

A college scholarship winner believed those words would help her get through a test she did not study for. But she never made it to the test. The few hits of crack killed her.

You can "overdose *dead* on crack," some people warn. This means you may not have to wait until your body breaks down from crack to die. Your first experience with it could be your last. Crack is a form of cocaine and is more addicting than other drugs. Some people become instantly hooked or instantly dead.

Other drugs you may have heard of or have experimented with are heroin, PCP, amphetamines, barbiturates, and tranquilizers.

Whether you use marijuana, cocaine, or other substances, the drug will not affect you the same way. There are many reasons for this, including how pure the drug is and how much of the drug you took. So if the kid who sits next to you has used drugs for a month without any outward signs the drug is affecting his mind and body, it does not mean you should start experimenting. It could mess you up for life.

Most experts agree that regular use of drugs blurs reality and helps people escape their problems. But this escape is only temporary. So if you use drugs to escape your problems instead of solving them, you will have to keep using more and more drugs to escape whatever you are running from.

Millions of kids do not use drugs, legal or illegal. Maybe this is because they are afraid of what drugs can do to their body. But they probably do not use them because they have found more exciting and constructive things to do than get stoned out of their head.

The more you know about yourself and the better you relate to others, the smaller the chance that you will be attracted to drugs. The odds skyrocket in your favor when you hang out with people who do not use them. So choose your friends carefully.

The bad news about drugs is that no one expects drug use to disappear completely. The good news is that young people are using legal and illegal drugs less than young people have used them in recent years. This does not mean drug use will never increase again. But, for now, it means there is less acceptance of drugs by young people and less peer pressure to use them.

SEXUALLY TRANSMITTED DISEASES

Most sexually transmitted diseases (STDs) have been around for centuries. They are usually caused by sexual intercourse between males and females and between people of the same sex. They can also be transmitted by drug users using dirty hypodermic needles and by women passing the diseases to their unborn children.

Gonorrhea is mentioned in documents that date as far back as 3,500 B.C. and it is still one of the most common sexually transmitted diseases. Symptoms of gonorrhea usually appear within a week after infection. Males may not show signs of the disease. If they do, the signs are a puslike discharge from the penis or an inflammation of the tube that carries urine from the kidney to the bladder. Females may not show symptoms, either. But signs may be a puslike discharge in the urine, itching, redness of the female glands, and pain in the abdomen.

Syphilis has also been around for a long time. Some people believe they have found its symptoms mentioned in the Bible. Roman emperors and English kings were said to be infected, and sailors who sailed with Christopher Columbus have been accused of bringing syphilis to Europe. But other people claim the disease was in Europe before Columbus came back from his voyages.

The disease has three stages. The first lasts between two to four weeks. During the first stage, an open sore appears in the genital area. After ten to fourteen days, the sore disappears. The second stage develops two to four weeks after the end of the first stage. During the second stage, there will be a fever, a rash, and a sore throat. There may be vomiting and loss of weight.

Symptoms can disappear for several years. But there is a third stage and it shows up three to five years after the first stage of infection. At this stage, the disease can cause heart, muscle, and bone damage and eventually can damage the brain.

Herpes causes cold sores, fever blisters, and other virus-related diseases. One of these is genital, or venereal, herpes. Venereal herpes is usually transmitted by sexual contact. But in some cases, venereal herpes may be passed from one person to another from infected clothes or other articles used by someone with venereal herpes.

After a person has been infected, it usually takes up to a week for fluid-filled sacs to show up on the sex organs. The sacs are painless until they break and cause open sores. Herpes may cause fever, exhaustion, and painful urination. Even though these symptoms will diminish and eventually disappear, this virus stays in your body for life.

AIDS is a "recent" disease. There are several theories about where it started. Some scientists think the virus existed thousands of years ago in areas of the world where people were not in contact with others. Others think natives of Africa became infected when they were bitten by green monkeys. Whatever the origin of AIDS, the first medically documented cases were found in San Francisco and New York in 1981. Because the two patients and other infected people were homosexual males, doctors thought only homosexual males carried the disease. Their thinking changed when AIDS showed up in all segments of the population. Now, thousands of people become unknowingly infected every day with the virus that causes AIDS.

AIDS, or acquired immune deficiency syndrome, reduces the body's ability to fight infections. This virus is called human immunodeficiency virus (HIV). It does not swirl around in the air. And it is not on the things you touch. So you cannot get AIDS by sharing pizza, books, phones, or anything else with a person who has the virus. And you do not get it if a person infected with AIDS breathes or sneezes on you or if you get tackled in a football game by somebody who carries the virus.

Some symptoms of HIV infection include fever, chills, diarrhea, swollen or tender lymph glands in the neck, jaw, armpit, or groin, and skin discoloration. Some people with AIDS become ill within weeks or months after infection. Others can be infected for 8 years or longer before showing symptoms. An infected mother can pass it to her child. Infection can also happen if you share a blood-tainted needle used by someone who has the disease. And you can get it while having unprotected sexual intercourse.

⚜ PROTECTING YOURSELF

There are many decisions in your life that are made for you by adults. But except in certain circumstance, like rape, you can make the decision to protect yourself against communicable diseases. You are the one who can decide the consequences of using a blood-tainted needle that somebody just pulled out of his arm. You are the one who can decide to have sexual intercourse or not to have it.

So before you decide to use needles or have sex, ask yourself why you want to do it. Is it because "everybody is doing it?" Is the person you are going with pressuring you? Do you feel you are weird because you are not using drugs or having sex? Answer these questions carefully. You will have to live with the consequences of your decision.

Abstinence from illegal drugs that enter your body through needles, and abstinence from sexual intercourse are the safest ways to protect yourself from communicable diseases. Thousands of kids who were sure they would not get these diseases are now infected.

There is nothing wrong in saying NO to drugs. And there is nothing wrong with you if you put off having sex. Sex is a big step and lots of kids are not ready for it, or they are not willing to gamble with their health and their lives.

If you decide to have sex, use a condom which is a thin rubber cover for the penis. You can buy condoms in drugstores or other convenience stores. Some health clinics will give you condoms. And at some schools, you can get them from the nurse. Do not depend on your partner to have condoms. Carry some with you. But even if you use a condom, you are not 100 percent safe. Condoms can be defective or they can break during intercourse. So abstinence is your only 100 percent guarantee.

For help to cope with health hazards, whether the health hazard belongs to you or to a friend, talk to an adult you trust. If you do not feel comfortable talking to someone you know, look in the phone book for social services and welfare organizations, community counseling, and adolescent crisis services. Or ask your telephone operator for the number of an organization that can help with your particular problem. There is help. You do not have to fight alone.

VII

NOBODY'S PERFECT

"What are you worrying about? You have your whole life ahead of you."

Adults often say this to teenagers, but although you may be thinking about your future, you are living for today. And sometimes today is hard to get through.

"What's the matter with teenagers today?"

The world that teenagers live in today is very different than the world teenagers lived in years ago. But teenagers are not very different. They still deal with a body that seems to change every week. Not only are the changes noticeable physically, they are also noticeable emotionally.

You are more restless. You often think people do not understand you. Especially your parents. What's their problem? Their problem may be that they forgot what it was like being a teenager. Then there is guilt. Theirs and yours. They feel guilty because they yell at you. You feel guilty because you yell at them.

And there is independence. Sometimes you think you are ready to take on the world. Other times you think the world is taking you on and pulverizing you. Face it. Not all that long ago, your biggest responsibility may have been to get a passing grade in school. Now, not only do you have to get a passing grade, you have to think about getting a job, registering for college, or going out on your own.

There are days when you want to pull the blankets over your head and shut out the world. Knowing that thousands of people feel that way may not make you feel better. But knowing that nothing stays the same, and today may be the day things change, should give you the courage to get out of bed.

Do not *just* get out of bed. Open your mind. Why is that person looking at the fast-food menu like he never saw it before? Make up a story about him. Maybe he only has a certain amount of money. Maybe he has a lot of money and he is trying to figure out what the homeless man down the street would like to eat. Maybe he is going to rob the place as soon as all the customers leave. Playing the "maybe" game will not solve all your problems. But it will get your mind off of them. And it may inspire you to write a story for extra credit in your English class.

"I'm afraid of having to play football against a 300 pound dude, of being run over by the girl I love, of the sky falling, of going to sleep with the light off."

This person has a lot of fears. You probably do too. So as long as you are out of bed, you may as well try to conquer a fear that keeps you from having fun or doing something that will help your present or future life. Start with something that you are only a little afraid of doing. Something little to you may be something big to somebody else. Maybe you think bungee jumping out of a hot-air balloon is a piece of cake, but meeting somebody new gives you the shakes. If eating snails is your favorite

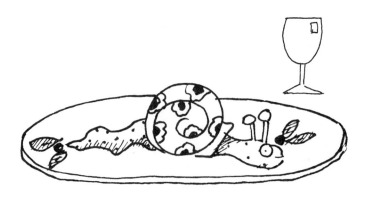

thing, you will not gag when you see one on your plate at your brother's wedding dinner.

But asking a guy to a dance may gag up your throat, and the words will not come out. So you decide which fear you should conquer. After you conquer one, conquer another. Fear of something new can keep you in a rut and not feeling good about yourself.

Evaluate yourself. Few people are totally satisfied with themselves, so do not put yourself down. What don't you like about yourself? Your looks? Your family? Your clothes? Your friends or lack of them? Which of these can you change? Which of these are you stuck with? Write an autobiography. Be honest but do not be too hard on yourself. Nobody is great at everything.

So focus on the things you like about yourself, and try to change the things you do not like. Be tolerant of your mistakes. Everybody makes them. And be open to new ideas, but do not let other people control your life.

You have some responsibilities to the adults in your life. After all, if you are under age according to the law, these people are the ones who will be in trouble if they do not control you. But the law will not hold your peers responsible if you get in trouble. So there is no reason to let them control your life.

Be your own person. Needing the constant approval of others and allowing them to make all or most of the decisions for you, shows that you do not feel good about yourself. If you do not always need the approval of your peers, or you do not always let them make decisions for you, this is a sign that you feel pretty good about yourself.

⋙ PEER PRESSURE

Everybody wants love and acceptance. And having a lot of friends is a way of having both. But choose carefully. If the people you think are friends hang around only because you help them with their homework, you have the best car on campus, and you give a party at your house every weekend, you may be as lonely as you would be if you were alone in your room watching Bugs Bunny cartoons.

Think of the party where the music blared, people danced in your living room, in the den, on the patio, some even danced in the pool, and no matter how much food the kids ate, your parents brought out more. And you felt lonely. The loneliness lasted only a moment. But in that moment, you realized nobody was talking to you or even paying attention to you. Sometimes you can be as lonely in a crowd as you would be alone. When this happens, ask yourself if the people around you like you or if they like what you can do for them.

Fear of rejection is something teenagers deal with all the time. Rejection is something that will happen to you during your whole life. But in high school, the need to belong becomes a craving that often leads teenagers to do something that can mess them up physically and emotionally.

89

Research shows teens who are totally influenced by peer pressure think less of themselves and their ability to do things. So to give themselves confidence, these kids hook onto people who seem to have everything going for them. Or they hook onto kids who are failing and who think breaking the law is their right.

Many teenagers feel their peers have affected their lives more than their families. Because of their peers, they experimented with drugs or did not experiment with drugs. They shoplifted or they did not shoplift. They cheated on tests or they did not cheat on tests. Their peers helped them through shattered loves, failing grades, and helped them get through family problems. Having friends gives you confidence and helps you feel good about yourself.

"I'm afraid of not making friends. Then I'll have to eat lunch by myself and I'll be an outcast."

To have friends, you have to be a friend. Do not always think that things have to be done your way, or people have to go where you want to go or do what you want to do. Do not act like you know everything. Show interest in people. Say something nice. Get involved with activities outside of school, which will enlarge your circle of friends.

☆ TEASING

Try not to show that teasing bothers you. Knowing why people tease may help you handle it. Are they jealous? Maybe they feel inferior around you. Lots of kids try to make themselves feel superior by making other people feel inferior. Maybe they are just having a bad day. Or maybe they really do not like you. Everybody in the world does not have to like you

Maybe they do like you. Then why do they tease you? Some people have a hard time giving compliments. How many times have you teased somebody because it was easier to say something negative than to say something positive?

The next time somebody teases you, ask yourself if that person's opinion is important to you. Should you accept the teasing without saying anything? Are you going to let the teasing get you down? If you do not let it get you down, the teaser has no control over you. If you let the teaser get you down, that person has control over you.

The way you handle teasing will show how you feel about yourself. You can laugh and not show the teasing bothers you. You can tell the person how the teasing makes you feel. You can ask for an apology. Or you can walk away. You have the right to express your feelings, whether they are expressed with words or with the action of walking away.

Sometimes how you handle teasing depends on what you are being teased about and how you feel about the person who is doing the teasing. For instance, if a girl who just broke up with you teases you about the way you kiss, emotionally you will handle the teasing differently than you will handle the teasing if the kid in the chow line says he does not like your shirt. If your brother teases you and you think your parents like him better than they like you, his teasing will bother you more than if you thought your parents liked you better than they like him.

✈ UNREALISTIC EXPECTATIONS

Nobody has all the answers. Life is not a math formula you can use to solve all your problems. For instance, you may be a 4.0 student but you may strike out every time you come to bat during gym. Or you cannot carry a tune. Or no matter how much you brush your hair, it looks like you had to walk through a typhoon to get to school.

Trying to do too much and trying to satisfy too many people can burn you out. Expecting too much from yourself can also keep you from trying something new. If you are afraid to fail, you will lose out on a lot of new experiences. Learning something new is how you grow as a person.

Failure also helps you grow as a person. So it is okay to mess up. What is not okay is giving up. So believe in yourself. You will be surprised what you can do!

APPENDIX 1
YOU HAVE SOME RIGHTS

Everybody is expected to obey laws. You may not always like the way things are, legally. But without laws, the world would be like a computer game gone crazy.

Adults decide what movies you can see, when you can drive, and when you can stop going to school. You may think this is not fair, but it is the law. And until you reach the age of majority, you must obey your parents.

Your parents may be your biological mother and father, your mother alone or your father alone. It may be your biological father and stepmother or your natural mother and stepfather. It may be an adoptive parent or an aunt and uncle. It could be a guardian who is given the job by the courts. Maybe your family is a group of people who have no biological relationship to you. Whatever your definition of family, everyone in the family has rights.

WHAT ARE YOUR RIGHTS AT SCHOOL?

You have the right to a free education. In return for that free education you must obey the rules of the schools.

Teachers and principals have the right to make you leave a room for disrupting a class, keep you after school, and if your state allows, to use physical punishment. But the punishment must be "humane and reasonable."

If you do not obey the rules, school administrators can take you off the sports teams, out of the school play, and keep you from other activities. You can even be expelled.

You have the right to defend yourself. If, after you meet with your school administrators, you still believe you have been unfairly punished, you have the right to go to the school board. If you feel the people at the school board are also unfair, you have the right to go to court.

You have the right to freedom of speech. This freedom includes actions as well as speech.

You have the right to style your hair the way you want and wear what you want as long as the way you are groomed does not interfere with the education of other students.

You have the right to go to school even if you have a disability.

In some states, you have the right to go to the public school of your choice.

In some states, you have the right to go to school even though you are pregnant or have a baby.

In some states, you have the right to go to school even though you are married.

⇴ WHAT ARE YOUR RIGHTS AT HOME?

Your parents have the right to control you. They can decide where you live, where you go to school, what religion you practice, how many hours you can be gone from home, and the friends you hang out with.

You have the right not to be morally, physically, or psychologically abused.

You have the right to shelter, food, clothing, and proper medication.

Because your parents must legally give you these, they have the right to collect all the money you make, unless you are self-supporting. But they do not have the right to make you work before you reach the legal working age in your state. And they do not have the right to make you work more hours than the law allows.

You have the right to emancipation. If you and your parents agree that you can support yourself, you can be emancipated, even if you are still a minor.

You can also be emancipated if you marry and you are not dependent on your parents for support, if you join the armed forces, or if you reach the age when the law considers you an adult.

APPENDIX 2

COLLEGE BOUND

Take control of your life. This is especially important if you want to get into the college of your choice.

Soon after you begin high school, make an appointment with your counselor. He will work out a schedule of the classes you need to get into college.

Keep in touch with him. Ask him questions. He has answers that will help you make decisions about your future.

Keep your grades up. Colleges study grades the way batters study fastballs.

Take Advanced Placement (AP) classes.

Take extracurricular activities. Sports, student newspapers, student government, and community services are some of the activities that look good on your college application.

Take the Preliminary Scholastic Aptitude Test/ National Merit Scholarship Qualifying Test (PSAT/ NMSQT). The PSAT is a practice run for the Scholastic Aptitude Test (SAT). It is usually taken in the fall of your junior year. You do not have to take the PSAT. But it will help you see what your strengths and weaknesses are. Another reason for taking the PSAT is that if you are one of the high scorers, you will be eligible for National Merit Scholarships.

Take the SAT. Prepare. Use the practice materials that come with your SAT registration packet. Your school library may have study guides. If your school gives SAT prep courses, take them or hire a private tutor.

Another test that is accepted by many colleges is the American College Testing Assessment Test (ACT). Some colleges require this test, and some accept it as an alternative to the SAT.

Go to college fairs and talk to college recruiters who come to your school. Study their brochures.

Write for admissions and financial aid information.

Visit campuses. Talk to teachers. Talk to students. What do they like about the school? What do they hate? Are the buildings close enough together so you will not have to be a long-distance runner to get to your next class on time? Is the equipment state of the art? How are the libraries?

Fill out college applications and write your essay. Think about it. Outline it. Write it. Rewrite it. Your essay is an important part of your application.

Get letters of recommendation to send with your application. Give brag sheets to the people who agree to write the letters. Brag sheets should tell what you like to do, what you are good at, and what you want to accomplish in life.

Have an alternate college in case you do not get your first choice. If you do not get your first choice, keep in mind the admissions people did not turn you down personally. There are many reasons why an application is rejected. Many colleges do not have room for every student who applies. This may be the reason you were not accepted at your first choice college.

In school, as in life, it is smart to have alternate plans. Maturity is taking what life gives you and turning it around. So, although rejection may seem like the end of the world, it is not.

Life throws curves. It is how you handle the curves that makes you the person you are.

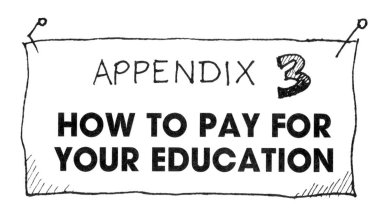

APPENDIX 3
HOW TO PAY FOR YOUR EDUCATION

You do not have to be from a low income family to qualify for student aid. But you must have financial need. The need is the difference between the cost of the school you will attend and what you and your family are expected to contribute to your education.

Federal and state government aid is given through grants, scholarships, loans, and work-study. Grants are usually based only on financial need. But sometimes grades are considered before a final decision is made. For scholarships, grades play an even more important part than they do for grants. Other considerations are talent, academic interest, and special background.

Social and church organizations, businesses, labor unions, professional societies, and foundations are some of the sources for educational funds.

There are a variety of school bank loans. Students who are independent from their parents have to reveal to the lender what they and their spouse (if there is one) own. Dependent students have to include what their parents own. These loans eventually have to be repaid with interest.

Work-study is part of your financial aid package. The school you enroll in helps you get a job with flexible hours so you can work around your class schedule.

Your school counselor will have information about how and where to apply for financial aid. Libraries also have books that give this kind of information. There are deadlines for applying for financial aid. Do not miss them!

You can pay for your education by joining the U.S. Armed Forces. If full-time active duty is more than you want, you can be on part-time active duty by joining the reserves of any armed forces.

You can pay for your education by getting a job. The age you can get papers that allow you to work depends on the state you live in.

When you apply for a job, dress neatly. Fill in all the spaces on the job application. If there are spaces that do not apply to you, write N/A, which means "not applicable".

First impressions are important. If you look sloppy, the person interviewing you may think you will be sloppy on the job. Say hello to the interviewer. Shake her hand. Sit straight. Look her in the eye. Do not smoke or chew gum, and do not fidget. Look interested in what this person has to say.

Some of the questions the interviewer will ask are: Why do you want to work? Have you worked before? How many hours a week can you work? What kind of work do you want to do when you graduate from school? Do you like school? What are your favorite subjects? How are your grades? Be truthful.

You can ask questions, too. What kind of work will you be doing? What hours will you have to work? What are the chances for promotion? How much money does the job pay? Ask this question last. The person you talk to knows you want to make as much money as possible. But employers need people who want to work for them, not only collect a paycheck.

Before you leave, thank the interviewer, whether you get the job or not. This will show you are courteous, and she may call you the next time there is a job opening.

APPENDIX 4

ORGANIZATIONS AND HOT LINES

AIDS Action Council
Federation of AIDS-Related Organizations
729 8th St. S.E., Suite 200
Washington, D.C. 20003
(202) 547-3101

Alcoholics Anonymous
P.O. Box 459
Grand Central Station
New York, N.Y. 10163
(212) 686-1100

Alcohol & Drug Problems Assn. of North America
444 North Capitol Street N.W., Suite 706
Washington, D.C. 20001
(202) 737-4340

American Council for Drug Education
5820 Hubbard Drive
Rockville, Md. 20852

Centers for Disease Control
1-800-443-0366

Drug Information Association
P.O. Box 3113
Maple Glen, Pa. 19002
(215) 628-2288

National Association on Drug Abuse Problems
355 Lexington Avenue
New York, N.Y. 10017

National Clearinghouse for Alcohol Information
P.O. Box 2345
Rockville, Md. 20857

National Clearinghouse for Drug Abuse
   Information
P.O. Box 416
Kensington, Md. 20795

National Institute on Drug Abuse Helpline
(800) 662-HELP or (800) 843-4971

FOR FURTHER READING

Bly, Robert. *Family Secrets.* New York: Harper & Row, 1987.

Claypool, Jane, and Lorna Greenberg. *Alcohol and You.* rev. ed. New York: Franklin Watts, 1988.

Condon, Judith. *Pressure To Take Drugs.* New York: Franklin Watts, 1990.

Epstein, Rachel. *Eating Habits and Disorders.* New York: Chelsea House, 1989.

Feldman, Robert S. *Understanding Stress.* New York: Franklin Watts, 1992.

Galperin, Anne. *Nutrition.* New York: Chelsea House, 1990.

Gold, Mark S. *800-Cocaine.* New York: Bantam Books, 1984.

Graeber, Laurel. *Are You Dying for a Drink?* New Jersey: Messner, 1986.

Henningfield, Jack E. *Addiction.* New York: Chelsea House, 1985.

Hyde, Margaret O., and Elizabeth H. Forsyth. *AIDS, What Does It Mean To You?* New York: Walker & Co., 1987.

Johnson, Earvin ("Magic"). *What You Can Do to Avoid Aids.* New York: Times Books, 1992.

Landau, Elaine. *Why Are They Starving Themselves: Understanding Anorexia Nervosa and Bulimia.* New Jersey: Messner, 1983.

Lyttle, Richard B., and Frank Farrara. *How to Pay for College.* New York: Franklin Watts, 1985.

Newman, Susan. *You Can Say No To a Drink Or a Drug: What Every Kid Should Know.* New York: Putnam, 1986.

Robertson, Nan. *Getting Better: Inside Alcoholics Anonymous.* New York: William Morrow, 1988.

Scott, Kitty L. *My Fight for Life: I am a Teenage Anorexic.* New York: Vantage, 1991.

Shaw, Diana, *Make the Most of a Good Thing, You.* Boston: The Atlantic Monthly Press, 1986.

Silverstein, Herma. *Alcoholism.* New York: Franklin Watts, 1990.

———*Teenage and Pregnant.* New Jersey: Messner, 1988.

Ward, Brian R. *Alcohol Abuse.* New York: Franklin Watts, 1988.

⫸ COLLEGE GUIDES

Birnbach, Lisa. *New & Improved College Book.* New Jersey: Prentice Hall Press, 1992.

Fiske, Edward B. *The Fiske Guide To Colleges.* New York: Times Books, Random House, 1992.

Nemko, Martin. *How To Get an Ivy League Education at a State University.* New York: Avon Books, 1992.

Solorzano, Lucia. *Barron's 300.* Hauppauge, New York: Barron's Educational Series, 1992.

Yale Daily News. Ed. by staff. *The Insiders Guide To the Colleges.* New York: St. Martin's Press, 1992.

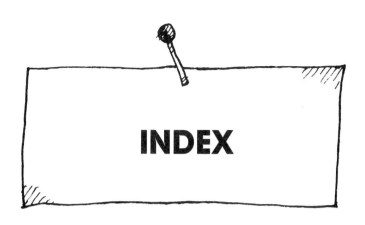

INDEX

ABOUT THE AUTHOR

Terry Dunnahoo wrote her first book in six weeks because an editor told her she could do it. Since Terry had never written anything except school essays, letters, and grocery lists, she believed six weeks must be how long it took to write a book. So she wrote 166 pages of finished copy in 42 days.

That first book was a biography about Nellie Bly. Biographies of Annie Sullivan and Emily Dunning quickly followed. Terry thinks talent is terrific, but discipline and determination are equally important. She used discipline and determination to write her first three books.

While she developed her talent, Terry never lost her discipline. The two led to 16 published books, which include a trilogy about a girl named Espie Sanchez. Her nonfiction books for Franklin Watts include *U.S. Territories and Freely Associated States, How to Win a School Election,* and *Pearl Harbor: America Enters the War.* She has won awards for her books, her teaching, and her contribution to the field of children's literature.

Terry is a longtime resident of Los Angeles and teaches writing at UCLA Extension. She also leads many smaller, informal writing workshops and writers' support groups, and spends as much time as she can with junior and senior high school students.